ART OF THE WESTERN WORLD

ITALIAN PAINTING
PERUGINO TO CARAVAGGIO

ANDREA EMILIANI

GOLDEN PRESS · NEW YORK

ART OF THE WESTERN WORLD

General Editor Marco Valsecchi

ITALIAN PAINTING: PERUGINO TO CARAVAGGIO

The paintings reproduced in this book were photographed by:
Crea: 5 — Istituto Geografico De Agostini: 2, 7, 11, 17, 18
Mella: 6, 15, 16, 19, 20, 21, 23 — Scala: 1, 3, 4, 8, 9, 10, 12, 13, 14, 22, 24.

Printed in Italy by Istituto Geografico De Agostini S. p. A. - Novara - 1963

INTRODUCTION

This volume presents a survey of the long and immensely productive era of Italian art which stretched from the beginning of the sixteenth century to the middle of the seventeenth. It was a period which saw the flowering of the High Renaissance, in the serenity and harmoniousness of Raphael's art; the burst of revolt and feverish experiment known as Mannerism; the austere attainments of the north-Italian schools of painting; the glorious blossoming of Venetian art; the revolutionary innovations of Caravaggio; and, finally, the vast, tumultuous achievement of the Baroque. An impressive range of activity indeed; and such as to make this one of the most fruitful and richly varied eras in the whole history of art.

In the development of Italian Renaissance art, the schools of painting of northern Italy played a distinctive and important role. Even in an age dominated by humanism the artists of the north stood out for the degree of their concern with human values and for their emotional intensity. The Renaissance arrived relatively late in the north. When it did arrive, it had to contend with the values of a society still largely feudal in outlook, and, in the artistic sphere, still committed to the style of International Gothic. The interaction that took place was as violent as it was fruitful, and we have only to consider the impact of Donatello's stay in Padua to appreciate this. The works that he executed there became the inspiration for all the best artistic minds of northern Italy; the great Mantegna, in particular, came under its powerful influence.

An important factor in the development of northern Renaissance art was the influence of the teacher and archaeologist, Francesco Squarcione. His studio in Padua became the centre of the new movement, transmitting the basic concepts and discoveries of the fathers of Renaissance art (Brunelleschi, Donatello, Masaccio), and assisting at the birth of radically new forms and ideas. Squarcione's most notable pupil was Mantegna; Mantegna, in turn, deeply influenced the painters of Ferrara and Lombardy. Squarcione himself produced little of value. His painting was both pedantic and sentimental, and he was too much concerned with style for its own sake. Mantegna, adapting the lessons of his teacher to his own purposes, forged a style of great power and individuality that became the model for the painters of Ferrara and Lombardy, notably Cosimo Tura. He also exercised a strong influence on the greatest Venetian artist of the fifteenth century, Giovanni

Bellini. The artists of northern Italy made full use of the technical discoveries of the Florentine masters, and they were quick to accept the notion of the central importance of the human figure. However, in contrast to the air of calm detachment that characterises the art of the Florentines, the work of these artists often conveys an effect of passionate involvement, and this is accentuated by the presence of strong regional elements.

To the formal, plastic and linear art of the Florentines, Venice opposed a free and vigorous expression, with colour as its most important element. In Ferrara and Bologna, stress was placed on a stylisation of a distinctly intellectual kind. In Lombardy, the new vision was grafted on to a tradition which contained the seeds of naturalism— seeds which were to come to full flower in the art of Lombardy's most celebrated painter, Michelangelo da Caravaggio.

The influence of Mantegna on Cosimo Tura has already been mentioned. Tura was also influenced by such artists as Pisanello, Jacopo Bellini, Roger van der Weyden and Piero della Francesca, all of whom he came into contact with as they passed through Ferrara on their visits to the Este court. It was thanks to Tura that Ferrarese painting acquired an independent and original character; before this, Ferrara had remained outside the major artistic movements of the day, limiting itself to following the example of its neighbours, Bologna and Venice. Yet although it largely partook of the values and chief styles of the Renaissance, Ferrarese painting sometimes seemed to hark back to the medieval world, in the way that it veered between spirituality and the depths of animal passion. The stylistic language achieved by Tura to the benefit of Ferrarese painting, which from then on was applied to the representation of objects of an incredible, unreal crystalline hardness, was a radical departure from the world of Tuscan

harmony. This language, which may be thought of as neo-Medieval, or perhaps pre-Mannerist, remained constant in all the painting of Tura's Ferrarese successors, from Francesco del Cossa—who was undoubtedly the most balanced of these violent artists—to Ercole Roberti, one of the few talents who approached the level of Giovanni Bellini in the point of 'modernity' of style and outlook, at the stage when humanism reached maturity.

In Bologna, the emotional and interpretative aspects of painting were gradually overlooked as more accent was placed on a classical style. This was especially the case with the lively and sensitive Lorenzo Costa—who from his youth was associated with Francesco Francia, a painter whose early strength became submerged in an excessive sentimentality. Bolognese art took quite a different direction in the work of Amico Aspertini, whose use of popular legends and stories, neglected since the fourteenth century, revived local anti-Roman prejudices in the artistic form of anti-classicism.

An intimate feeling for nature, which he depicted in the full range of its qualities of light and tone, led the Lombard Vincenzo Foppa to the invention of an original style, which pointed beyond the limits of Renaissance theory and practice in the direction of a radically new kind of painting. In his work the established canons of perspective and composition seemed to dissolve in a loving study of light. His followers continued to paint in his style until the arrival in Milan of Donato Bramante, who brought to the art of Lombardy an emphasis on naturalism, a new interest in perspective-spatial relationships. The heritage of this naturalism, the origins of which are to be sought in local fourteenth-century painting, was passed on to Bramante's pupil Ambrogio da Fossano, called Borgognone (whose work showed the influence of Flemish art as well) and it was passed on also to another Lombard artist of importance, the Milanese Carlo Braccesco. Great emphasis was placed on style in the work of Bernardino Butinone, which was partly influenced by Paduan painting and partly by the art of Bramante, and the climax of this stylism was to be found in the unreal and deeply intellectual classicism of Bramantino, which points towards Mannerism. With Bramantino, and with Leonardo's arrival in Milan, the great age of Lombard humanism seems, if only momentarily, to come to an end.

If the influence of the late Gothic tradition on Lombard Renaissance painters was strong and enduring, it was even more so in the case of Piedmontese painters such as Martino Spanzotti and Defendente Ferrari. In the work of both these painters, however, and particularly in that of Spanzotti, the powerful, if subdued, plastic quality obtained by means of light produced a lively and original effect, mingled with reminiscences of the Medieval world.

According to Vasari's celebrated remark, the art of the early years of the sixteenth century attained heights never before reached, and it was to set the pattern for every future development. It is clear that Vasari, himself a painter, and by general consent the founder of modern art criticism, did not mean his remark to imply only the acquisition of the means for a perfect representation of objects, but also the serene balance which artists achieved, in that period of intense creative activity, between man and the objects surrounding him. But this period was a brief one, and it was soon to be disturbed by the artistic crisis to which the name ' Mannerism ' has been given in modern times.

The period of classicism in Renaissance art is synonymous with that extraordinary maturity of humanist values which Bramante, Leonardo, Michelangelo and Raphael realised in their work. The Renaissance painters attained a perfect unity of composition which encom-passed the whole problem of space, while at the same time a deeper exploration of the natural brought into play all the formal, linear, chromatic and plastic resources at the artists' disposal. The unifying concepts which underlay all their work were those of a Platonic perfection and of the sovereign dignity of man. Until these ideas had hardened into clichés, they were the basic inspiration of all the best sixteenth century thought. They anticipated the modern idea of man as the supreme director of nature, who is continually seeking to modify and transfigure it. The great artists named worked to the same end, and to them we may add Titian's classicism in ' chromatic ' key, rich in its intimate strength, and more enduring.

Without wishing to succumb to the temptations and the ingenuities of historical determinism, it should be pointed out that the greatest years of Renaissance classicism coincide with the beginning of the political misfortunes of Italy, and the outbreak of the conflicts which had been gathering momentum since the last years of the fifteenth century. It should not be overlooked that the Renaissance as manifested in Michelangelo, for example, was not the same as the Renaissance which appeared in the art of his contemporary, Raphael, with its sublime harmony between idea and nature; and that Leonardo, with his profound scepticism, resembled neither. The first upset in the equilibrium of the Renaissance was caused by Michelangelo's *Tondo Doni* (now in the Uffizi Gallery), which he painted in the early years of the century. For Raphael, the crisis arose in the middle of the second decade of the century, and it caused him to turn away from painting in the last years of his life. The earliest avowed Mannerists, from Beccafumi to Berruguete, had already been active for for some years. An unsuspected, almost unimaginable crisis revealed itself, a crisis which was to have the most profound repercussions. The crisis showed itself in a growing disquiet, rather than in open revolt. It arose from the formulae of classicism itself, which almost immediately became static and abstract in response to the new demands of expression. This disquiet, which expressed itself in the urge to pass beyond the canon of a lost perfection, carried with it the consciousness that the perfect and almost mystical circle of the formal art of mature humanism must not be broken. Today Mannerism is understood as a struggle initiated from within rather than as an attack from outside. To say Mannerism was a period of anti-classical anarchy is repeating an old prejudice, especially as the works of the greatest Mannerists show nothing which offends against the Renaissance canons of formal perfection. What does show is a feeling of exasperation at the need to remain imprisoned within them.

Mannerism was not a simple phenomenon. It contained within itself a diversity of moods and styles: from the hallucinatory grace of Rosso Fiorentino to the powerful naturalism of Pontormo, from the cold introversion of Bronzino to the extraordinary metaphorical art of Parmigianino. When the movement was at its height, the Emilian painter Correggio opposed resistance to this new relationship between intellect and sensuality: his intimately Lombard version of classicism was destined, by way of reaction to the prevalent unrest, to become the most highly valued model of seventeenth-century classicism.

It is to the credit of twentieth-century art criticism that it has ' discovered ' the Baroque. The Baroque is now appreciated as much for its historical importance as for its artistic achievements. It was the Baroque which first expressed certain modern aesthetic truths, including that of the organic connection between the different arts. It produced

the concept of the dignity of individual artistic work, freeing the artist from the status of mere craftsman. The relation between pupil and master changed as the concept of plagiarism—of such importance in Romantic aesthetics—replaced the concept of liberty in imitation. These attitudes were fundamental to the new thinking of the century, with its anxieties and over-abundance of vitality, its sudden abandonings and deliberate desecrations. It could not be confined by the limits of a serene philosophy, within an ordered and closed concept of rational harmony. A new dynamism of spirit and senses, a vital and positive irrationality, suddenly became allied to the first fruits of scientific research—that is, to a new vision of universal infinity—and led man beyond the limits of his own creation to a world which was the mirror of his own vitality. Seventeenth-century man soon found himself enveloped by ' multiple visions on different planes of contrasting systems, in a sort of systematic multipolarity ' (Anceschi).

We need not concern ourselves with the present state of the Baroque controversy—it is often more aesthetic than historical. We can see that certain characteristics, which recur so frequently as to appear constant, underlie the various experiments of the century. A great variety of moral and spiritual trends developed throughout Europe, almost a *discors concordia* of trials and experiments. The great difficulty of recognising a common basis for all these tendencies can readily be appreciated. It would be more fruitful to consider, within the ambit of a strictly historical perspective, the three main directions of this movement, and to distinguish the contribution of the countries which played the greatest part in seventeenth-century culture. Among the diverse ideological and spiritual constants proposed as the basis for the stylistic unity of the Baroque, the most acceptable would appear to be Briganti's, to whom scholars owe the most profound portrayal of that period: 'The most appropriate historical perspective will be that of the new feeling for nature which arose from the liveliest seventeenth-century thought: that feeling which, repudiating the theological concept of the world, produced a new awareness of the infinity of the spirit, matter and conscience, which so often became coloured with poetry and caused a mysterious dismay to enter the highest minds of the century. Nature itself is no longer imagined as the realm of man and the motionless outward reflexion of an internal order, but is now realised as infinite space, freed from visible and invisible forces, so much more vast and unknown than that circumscribed " star-studded bowl " which man had until then believed it to be.' This interpretation is a synthesis of the literary and philosophical experiments of the century. When the Aristotelian-Thomistic philosophy first fell into disfavour and Galileo's discoveries brought the new world into being, a new feeling emerged for nature ' in whose newly realised infinity man finds himself, no longer in a world directed by his own conscience, but one in which he appears relegated to the role of spectator ' (Anceschi).

Today most of the heat once generated by the subject has died down and the derogatory meaning of the term 'Baroque' has largely disappeared. If we re-read today the words of Milizia, an eighteenth-century writer violently opposed to the Baroque, we will find the outlook that was typical of that century: referring to Borromini, he states that this architect of genius ' carried extravagance to the highest degree of delirium. He deformed every shape, mutilated façades, turned volutes inside out, cut off corners, brought undulations to architraves and cornices, and employed a profusion of cartouches, snails, zigzags and all sorts of odds and ends. Borromini's architecture is an architecture in reverse. It is not architecture, it is a fantastic carpenter's jumble. Borromini in architecture, Bernini in sculpture, Cavaliere Marini in poetry, are the plagues of good taste. Plagues which have infected a great number of artists. But there is no evil which cannot give rise to good. It is good to see their works, and to abominate them. They serve to show us what should not be done. They are to be considered criminals, who endure punishment for their crimes in order to serve as instruction for reasonable beings.' The reader of today cannot fail to perceive that the basis of this extreme condemnation of the Baroque can also be the basis for a positive interpretation.

But it would seem timely to lay greater stress than has hitherto been the case on the lack of a strong unifying principle determining the direction of these diverse artistic manifestations. For the distance which separates Caravaggio from Pietro da Cortona, or even from Annibale Carracci, appears so great that a basic principle needs to be sought. After three centuries of heated debate, the term ' Baroque ' should now be restored to its original meaning. That is, ' Baroque ' must be taken to signify that moment in the history of the seventeenth century—around the year 1630—when there were gathered together in Rome the principal participants in an event which marked the climax and maturity of the new movement. It should be used to refer to the generation of Pietro da Cortona, Borromini, Bernini and Poussin; a very different generation, and conditioned by quite different forces, from that generation which first appeared at the opening of the seventeenth century, and tried with varying success to effect reforms or revolutions; very different, that is, from the generation of Caravaggio, Rubens and the great Italian and north-European followers of Caravaggio, and different too from the Carracci, with their romantic attitude to the great Italian pictorial tradition of ' historical romance.' How far the so-called Roman Baroque of 1630 had travelled from its original outlook is shown by its departure from the most important belief of the century, the belief in natural truth, which Caravaggio had held in common with Bruno, Campanella and Galileo. In the all-embracing folds of triumphant Catholicism, the men of the Baroque turned aside from the cold severity of the early reformers, such as the melancholy Lodovico Carracci in Bologna, and also from the followers of Caravaggesque naturalism.

As the century progressed, it grew farther and farther away from what had been its most fundamental intuitions, which had all been expressed within the first thirty years. The feeling of security and the domination of the Church over all spheres of development after the Counter-Reformation, exerted a strong influence on artistic expression, which came to mean inventive originality, both dramatic and ingenious. So the terms of sacred art began to undergo a profound change; they had previously been rigorously orientated towards Puritanism by Council of Trent, but now the conquest of new worlds and the establishment of the missions made it possible for an infinite number of beliefs and dogmas to arise. As a consequence, vast new opportunities opened up for the artist.

A more elegant and harmonious art made its appearance at the end of the seventeenth-century. It found its expression in the language, soon to become international, of ' Rococo.' The new style became very widespread in the course of the eighteenth-century, passing from court to court, and gathering on its way more decorativeness than substance. The contrast which had been the fundamental theme of the whole preceding century grew less marked, and with the age of light came the birth of a new rationalism, a renewal of faith in the importance of human relations, and new art forms no longer based on extreme contrasts of colour and composition, but on a wish to give precise expression to the real. The best achievements of eighteenth century art, at least in Italy, are to be found in that vast area of naturalism which was inhabited by painters of society such as Pietro Longhi, Ceruti, Traversi and Crespi of Bologna, and the more intimate, light-filled works of such great artists as Canaletto and Bellotto.

THE PLATES

Plate 1—COSIMO TURA: Saint Anthony of Padua. This starkly majestic figure of St Anthony epitomises the calm strength and severity of purpose of the first important Renaissance painter of Ferrara, Cosimo Tura. Each feature of the painting expresses a firm and clear intention, from the colours, which seem to derive from the imagination of the artist rather than from reality, to the contorted forms and broken, writhing lines of the figure. The ornate and rigid architecture, and the restless landscape which it frames, serve to accentuate the drama of the figure as well as to place it in perspective. This painting displays Tura's characteristically rugged and powerful structural quality. His genius is far removed from the mental contortions of Mannerism.

The painting, now in the Galleria Estense in Modena, was probably the central section of a larger composition, perhaps a polyptych, painted in 1484 for Francesco Nasello, who was secretary to the Duke of Ferrara, Ercole I d'Este. Tura, an old and tired man, wrote to Nasello in 1490, asking him for a payment of 60 scudi for having 'six years ago made at my own expense an alterpiece of gold and colours which is in San Nicolò in Ferrara'. To emphasise his dire need, the great painter

added: 'I do not know how I can manage to live and sustain myself in this way since I have no profession or faculty to support myself and my family... being very ill.'

Cosimo Tura was born in 1430. He witnessed the 'events' connected with the diffusion of Renaissance art through northern Italy, notably Donatello's stay in Padua, Roger van der Weyden's visit to Ferrara, and Piero della Francesca's journey through the north in the middle years of the century. 'Squarcionism' —the artistic movement in Padua which first reaped the benefits of Tuscan achievement— she wed itself at its best in the altar of the Santo Church. Yet it soon broke away from the influence of Tuscany and acquired its own creative personality, as harsh as it was inaccessible. By the side of it and following the same direction, a school of miniaturists and painters arose in Ferrara, all of whom aimed at giving form to a new world of human truth, as Leon Battista Alberti showed with some of his works in the still essentially Gothic city.

In the work of Tura, there is from the earliest period until the last years of his life, a firm strength which rarely wavers, and a hitherto almost unknown energy which he hurled into every one of his works, with an unchanging

Plate 1. COSIMO TURA (Ferrara, 1430-1495): *St Anthony of Padua*. Tempera on panel, 154 x 80 cm. Modena, Galleria Estense.

Plate 2. ERCOLE ROBERTI (Ferrara, 1450?-1496):
The Miracles of St Vincenzo Ferreri (Detail). Tempera on panel. Rome, Vatican Gallery.

method and violence of feeling. Tura influenced, directly or indirectly, all the other painters of Ferrara, from Cossa to Roberti: it was probably to them that he entrusted the execution of the frescoes in the Room of the Months in the Palazzo di Schifanoia in Ferrara, which, although not painted by his own hand, yet suggest in their unity of conception the influence of his powerful, inventive mind.

Plate 2—ERCOLE ROBERTI: The Miracles of St Vincenzo Ferreri (*detail*). A tradition referred to by Vasari in the two *Lives* dedicated to Ercole Ferrarese and Lorenzo Costa (whom he took for the same person as Francesco del Cossa), holds that this predella, formerly standing below the Griffoni family's altar in the Church of San Petronio, Bologna, was the work of Ercole Roberti. Scholars have recently confirmed that the predella and four lateral Saints were the work of Ercole, and that Cossa, during his stay in Bologna, was responsible for the invention and much of the execution of the altarpiece (Longhi). Roberti, the younger (and some think greater) of the two geniuses of Ferrara, worked on the painting between 1475 and 1477, that is, a few years after the work had been begun by Cossa.

Born around the year 1450, Ercole Roberti found himself early in his career working on the scaffolding erected for the painters who were employed on the decoration of the Room of the Months in the Palazzo di Schifanoia in Ferrara. He was perhaps not yet twenty when he started work on the section called *September*. The style in which *September* was executed was certainly in advance of its time, and points to the emergence of a new artistic generation. It was Longhi who recognised that this harsh and tormented work was by the hand of Roberti, and to Longhi also we owe a most exact and illuminating study of the artist and the definitive catalogue of his works.

It was Ercole Roberti who raised Ferrarese art, which had been nurtured on Tura's hard and sharp forms, to the highest level of north-Italian art, and made Ferrara worthy to rank with her great neighbour, Venice. Ferrarese art had reached the limits of its expressive autonomy in the figures of Cosimo Tura and Francesco del Cossa. It was through Ercole Roberti that the later Ferrarese painters were able to benefit from that happy fusion of styles which Antonello da Messina and Giovanni Bellini wrought together upon the basis of Piero della Francesca's sublime formal synthesis. To those who were alert at that time, this stylistic union appeared as the most extraordinary cultural compact of the Renaissance; and few knew as well as the great Ferrarese how to absorb to the full the 'modernity' of the event without forgetting the grandeur of the past to which he belonged. Even after absorbing this new influence, Ercole Roberti did not renounce any of the characteristics peculiar to Ferrarese art.

In the detail illustrated here we can observe the painter's constant concern for expressiveness, which takes the form of a kind of determined 'cubization' of even the most fragmentary details. The archaeological details are accumulated one on the other in order to support the dynamic weight. The ruins of the house and the impassioned gestures of those putting out the fire show the most daring 'trompe-l'oeil' perspective which fifteenth century art had invented, with a continual breaking up of space, a spasmodic segmentation of line, creating volumes of boundless energy. And in this dynamic action the complex drama unfolds. The beams blackened by fire form a tragic and essential detail, and they serve to arrest, against a sky of crystalline hardness, the spiral movements that are arising from below.

Plate 3. PIETRO VANNUCCI called PERUGINO (Città della Pieve, c. 1448-1523): *Fortitude and Temperance* (detail of two Ancient Heroes). Frescoes, Perugia, Collegio del Cambio.

Jardinière, the Urbino Muta or the Deposition for Atalanta Baglioni, was quite sudden; and even today we are unable to state with certainty that it took place in 1508. Vasari suggests that the reason for his departure was Bramante's advice to Pope Julius II that he should employ the young and already famous Raphael in the decoration of his new apartments in the Vatican Palace.

In Rome Raphael found the Milanese Bramantino, Sodoma, Peruzzi and his own master Perugino already at work; and it is probable that he himself immediately set to work, although the first documentary evidence of his presence did not appear until January 1509. It is, however, certain that his rise to fame was very rapid, for within a very short time Julius II entrusted to him the whole decoration project, ordering him to destroy the works of the artists already commissioned so that he could be unhampered by their work. This resulted in the invention and execution of what may justly be described as the most famous fresco cycle in the history of painting.

The work began in the Stanza della Segnatura (which was intended to contain Pope Julius II's Library) and here many of the most celebrated figures of western civilisation were represented in unforgettable form, in the famous Disputa del Sacramento (The Discussion as to the Nature of the Sacrament), Parnassus, and The Virtues.

He then turned to the Stanza d'Eliodoro, for which work he received the final payment in August 1514.

This work has some political significance, and it is believed that Pope Julius II himself collaborated in it. Raphael was given the commission in 1511. In this room, on a wall where a broad window opens out, Raphael painted the episode of the Mass of Bolsena. The work recalls an episode which occurred in the small town of Bolsena in

Lazio, in 1263, when a priest saw blood drip from the host while Mass was being celebrated. (A similar occurrence was the origin of the annual feast of Corpus Domini.) The Pope kneels before the altar, with Cardinal Riario and Cardinal Sangiorgio in attendance. It is now believed by some historians that Lorenzo Lotto was responsible for a part of this work, as the group on the right shows a marked Venetian influence.

This Mass of Bolsena is one of the most extraordinary of Raphael's great works. It was probably painted in 1512 or soon after, and Raphael's invention of the great, mysterious pyramidal form of composition appears here for the first time, animating the vast composition with its elaborate organisation of space. Raphael appears to have been constricted by the window, and he had to adapt his composition because of it, placing the altar at the top of a double flight of steps. Set between sweeping curves of vast convex areas, a great arch encircles the whole composition, and the miraculous host, which is the centre of the action, assumes a grave and majestic character. It is the crown, as it were, of an astonished silence, which descended on all sides, merging into the deep concentration of the Pope's prayer, the meditation of the priests, and finally the sharp naturalistic treatment of the Swiss attendants. This last is a passage of extraordinary power, in which the chromatic structure is accompanied by an inventivenes almost d'après nature.

After the stanza d'Eliodoro, in which are also the famous Repulse of Attila and St Peter Delivered from Prison frescoes, Raphael began work on the Stanza dell'Incendio di Borgo (1514-17), and the Sala di Costantino, which Pope Leo X commissioned from him in 1517. Much of this work was in fact done by Raphael's pupils, who completed them after his death.

Plate 5. RAFFAELLO SANZIO (Urbino, 1483-1520): The Mass of Bolsena (detail). Fresco, Rome, Vatican Palace.

LEONIDA LACEDEMONIO · ORATIO COC

Plate 3—PIETRO VANNUCCI called PE-RUGINO: Fortitude and Temperance (*detail of two Ancient Heroes*). The origins of the Perugian Collegio del Cambio go back to the first half of the thirteenth century, but it was not until the fifteenth century that it was established in a permanent building. The Hall was built between 1453 and 1457, and the furnishings were ordered in 1490. In January 1496, the Council decided to entrust the pictorial decoration to Perugino, who was already a famous artist, while the humanist Francesco Maturanzio was to work out the themes of the subject and carry out the necessary negotiations with the artist.

The next date of interest is the year 1507, when the artist was paid for the work. From this many historians have inferred that the work itself was protracted beyond the beginning of the new century. However, stylistic evidence and also the evidence of certain external events reveal that the work, which was begun in 1497, must have been completed by the year 1500. Some of the painting was done by pupils, who are mentioned by Vasari. Later, a tradition arose to the effect that the young Raphael had a hand in some parts of the decoration, some saying that these can be recognised as his. In particular, Adolfo Venturi saw the hand of Raphael in the figure of Fortitude and in some other details, although these could hardly have been executed by Raphael before 1505. It seems, however, that the possibility of young Raphael being present and taking part in the decoration of the Collegio del Cambio is remote, since the style of these parts is practically indistinguishable from the style of the others, and is very closely related to that of the other pupils in Perugino's circle.

These are the most interesting years in the life of Perugino. He moved towards that ' rhythmical classicism ' which was to become more accentuated with the arrival in his studio of the young Raphael. Perugino was born at Città della Pieve in Umbria towards the middle of the century, the first certain reference to him appearing in 1478. Before he was nine, he was apprenticed to a painter in Perugia, apparently a mediocre artist but one ' with a sincere veneration for the great things in art '. He worked for a time in Arezzo, possibly under Piero della Francesca, and then went to Florence where he studied under Andrea del Verrocchio in company with Leonardo. One of his earliest works is a fresco, dated 1478, in the church of Castel Cerqueto, near Perugia, which shows a beautiful figure of St Sebastian. Verrocchio's influence is clearly visible in the beautiful Madonna in the Jacquemart-André Museum in Paris. Perugino was also an admirer of Botticelli and Pollaiuolo. From 1480-82 he worked in the Sistine Chapel in company with Pinturicchio, Ghirlandajo, and others, and produced a number of frescoes, *The Assumption*, *Moses in the Bulrushes*, and a Nativity. All were subsequently destroyed to make way for Michelangelo's *Last Judgement*.

When Perugino was about twenty-five he painted the famous *Stories of St Bernardino* which have only recently been definitely assigned to him Perugino's was essentially a rhythmical construction in the sense of the organisation of the relationship between figures and landscape. A marvellous harmony exists in his work. The figures are gently graceful and modest, the scenes bathed with soft evening light, and the composition flows with musical ease. Such was the legacy which the sixteen-year-old Raphael was to inherit when he arrived at Perugino's studio. It is ironical that although Pope Julius II commissioned the ageing and famous Perugino to decorate one of the Stanzie of the Vatican, that he was eventually to hand the job to Raphael instead, and Perugino retired from Rome, to return to his name-town, Perugia.

Plate 4—RAFFAELLO SANZIO (Raphael): The Betrothal of the Virgin. The work was painted for the Church of the Conventual Francescans in Città di Castello in 1504—as can be seen from the date inscribed on the temple front—and remained there until 1798 when it was yielded to Napoleon's General Lechi. It later hung in the Great Hospital in Milan, and in 1806 was bought for the Brera Gallery by the Viceroy Eugène de Beauharnais.

This early work of the young Urbino artist shows his close affinity with the art of Perugino, who had composed a similar subject for the Sistine Chapel in Rome. Yet at the same time there are substantial differences in style between the two works: the earlier was still related to a gracious and rhythmical, but not highly inventive, type of painting, while Raphael's was completely liberated, in its sublime spatial counterpoint between foreground and landscape.

It is known that the young artist was educated in Urbino. There, possibly through the mediation of his father Giovanni, himself a painter, he was in constant attendance at the Montefeltro court, where he absorbed its principal characteristics. The powerful figure of Piero della Francesca dominated here, and the very life of the city seemed to be gathered within that Palazzo del Laurana (one of the most sublime examples of the rhythmical arrangement of architectonic masses in the history of Western architecture). The recent addition of this youthful fresco to the Santi house in Urbino shows how Piero's vision was translated into the style of an adolescent of genius, the powerful synthesis of the former diluted into subtle modulations.

Similar works followed, the most significant being the Charity Standard in Città di Castello. Then, in 1496, came Perugino's summons to Raphael to join him in his studio and this—as we know not only from legend—turned out to be of decided advantage to the work of the older

painter. Raphael may have gone to Florence between 1496 and 1498, for already in those years the somewhat languid reflection of Perugino's painting in his work yielded to a clear and sharp naturalism derived from Della Robbia. In any event, he was working in Florence at the start of the new century, and spent more continuous periods of time there from 1504. In Florence he found a heated atmosphere centred around Michelangelo's dynamic *Tondo Doni*, painted at the high point of the Renaissance; while Leonardo was painting his *Gioconda* and preparing the project for Saint Anne. Raphael's mature work now began. He took themes from the history of Florence—which had been presented in condensed form by such painters as Lorenzo di Credi, Fra Bartolommeo and Piero di Cosimo—and thus the greatest attitudes of the past reappeared in his work.

With the *Madonna of the Grand Duke*, painted at the end of 1504, and his return to Perugia—where his unfinished works awaited him, among them the Colonna Altarpiece (Washington, Kress Collection) and the Ansidei Altarpiece (London, National Gallery)—the constant progression in his style evolved in the direction of an intimate harmony between form and feeling, to the point where he attained a profound and all-embracing humanity. We may discount the legends which have for so many years been built up around the artist and his miraculous youth, yet it is an undeniable fact that when he was but a little over twenty years of age, Raphael had already attained complete mastery of his art, and achieved a perfect equilibrium between reality and theory.

Plate 5—RAFFAELLO SANZIO: The Mass of Bolsena (*detail*). Raphael's departure from Florence, where he had just completed works like the *Madonna del Cardellino, La Belle*

Plate 4. RAFFAELLO SANZIO (Urbino 1483-1520):
The Betrothal of the Virgin (Sposalizio). Oil on panel, 170 x 118 cm. Milan, Brera.

Plate 6—RAFFAELLO SANZIO: La Fornarina. This famous woman has always been traditionally identified with Margherita, wife of Francesco Luti, a baker, of Santa Dorotes, who was known as La Fornarina and played so great a part in Raphael's real (and legendary) life. It is now the opinion of most scholars that Raphael had very little part in this work, except in one or two inconsiderable passages, and that the portrait is almost entirely the work of his pupil Giulio Pippi, known as Giulio Romano. Yet this portrait does enable us to understand Raphael's late work, as it was passed to his greatest pupil. It contained within it all the symptoms of ' Mannerism ', which was from then on to invade the world of the Renaissance, breaking up its perfect unity of feeling and style.

But to return to the last years of Raphael's life. In 1515 a Papal ' brief ' named him keeper of the ruins of Rome; and it seems now that his passion for archaeology—which began at the time of his greatest success when he had reached the climax of a vast programme of work—has some vital inner significance, whose final outcome we cannot fathom because of Raphael's premature death.

A thorough examination of Raphael's last works, especially now that the theoretical and historical notion of Mannerism has acquired an almost universally accepted meaning, would clarify many of the aspects of that late and unquiet Roman classicism which was of such great importance in the development of painting in the second half of the century.

The plan and execution of the cartoons for the Vatican tapestries belong to the last years of Raphael's life. His flowing eloquence—once thought to be mere rhetoric—is the climax of the ' grand manner ', and anticipates the European classicism, which was to emerge almost intact a hundred years later in a part-Romantic part-ideological form. Raphael's art, in common with the art of Annibale Carracci, Domenichino, Nicolas Poussin or Claude Lorrain, embraces all of history in the light of contemporary life.

Certain aspects of the portraits of the *Donna Velata* (Veiled Woman) and *Leo X* are of particular significance, in that they indicate Raphael's slow but inevitable evolution towards Mannerism: in the former there are passages in the treatment of the drapery which show marked innovation, in the latter there is a new understanding of the quality of light.

This infiltration of Mannerism became more marked in the later works (which are rather tentative, for example the so-called *Spasimo di Sicilia*, or *St Michael Archangel* in the Louvre), finally resolving itself in an episode of paramount importance for the history of Mannerist and Baroque classicism: the *Vision of Ezekiel* in the Pitti Palace. The hesitancy in this work may perhaps owe something to the influence of Michelangelo, with his combination of a powerful scepticism and iron will. Time was perhaps preparing further innovations for Raphael beyond his time, and we can now ponder them in the famous *Transfiguration* in the Vatican. This unfinished work was hung above Raphael's coffin; some new experiments can be observed, particularly in the conflict between the idealised vision and the new naturalistic treatment of light in the lower part of the altarpiece.

Plate 7—BERNARDINO LUINI: The Dispute with the Doctors (*detail*). The frescoes in the Saronno Sanctuary, a detail of which is illustrated here, are among the highest achievements of this Lombard painter's delicate art. They were painted around the year 1525, at a time when the Lombard Renaissance was well advanced.

In that region, where the mode of expression created by the fourteenth-century artists had developed an intimate, naturalistic vein, the last phase of Gothic civilisation was eventually to triumph. This ornate and lively art had spread widely throughout the West and became known as International Gothic. With the twilight of the Middle Ages, International Gothic became the vehicle of expression for the whole of northern Italy: but it was particularly strong in Lombardy, far from Padua and the other centres of humanistic culture, as if resisting the ideals of the Renaissance. It was as if the same tendency towards naturalism which had marked the beginning of the modern era in northern Europe, first in Van Eyck and soon after in Fouquet, was held to be more valid than the theorising of Tuscan and Umbrian art in central Italy. In Lombard art which was at times very ornate, at others charged with gentle emotion, there persisted the marks of a very different outlook from that of Tuscany, which was so much more rigorous. Lombard thought was always prone to wander off along its own paths of fantasy.

It was the Brescian artist Vincenzo Foppa, who, following the main-stream of northern humanism, that is, the humanism of Padua, brought an end to the luxuriant growth of cosmopolitanism in Lombard Gothic art, and introduced a note of simplicity and naturalism. He was less interested in perspective and classicism, and his simple and intimate style, even at the height of the Renaissance recalls the sharp naturalistic observation of earlier artists like Giovanni da Milano or Bonifacio Bembo.

Foppa's painting was spared the arid experiment and futile theorising which had led so many provincial artists astray; the realism of his paintings becomes narrative and domestic, expressed in a surprisingly advanced manner. It was due mainly to the arrival of Bramante in Milan that local painting developed a firmly independent version of the aesthetic theories which were typical of the Tuscan Renaissance. But if Foppa's pupil Bergognone continued to paint in a naturalistic manner, Bernardino Butinone and Bernardo Zenale sought to destroy the tender regard for things seen in a violent use of perspective. Bramantino was even more extreme; entirely within the classical ideal, he aimed at creating a world of proud beauty and rigid formalism, and achieved results of an almost metaphysical profundity.

The task of continuing these developments fell on Bernardino Luini, who reduced them to the scale of an ornate and graceful myth. With the arrival of Leonardo da Vinci in Milan, this ingenuous felicity—which others seemed to lack or at least added a note of sombreness to the pleasant naturalism of the Lombard tradition—did not diminish; for it was just at that time that such works as the *Madonna of the Rose Hedge* were produced. This picture, although it indicates Luini's inventive timidity, remains among the most charming examples of the more popular and attractive art of the time.

Plate 8—ANDREA DEL SARTO: The Sacrifice of Abraham. The life of this great Florentine master, who has recently been rather neglected but who played such a vital part in Florentine and central Italian sixteenth-century art, has been related in minute detail by Vasari. According to Vasari, he was first apprenticed to a goldsmith, and then became a pupil of Piero di Cosimo. Later, in his maturity as a painter, he was influenced by Fra Bartolomeo and Michelangelo.

Andrea del Sarto was called to France in 1518 by Francis I. Thus began that relationship which was to give France its Renaissance.

Plate 6. RAFFAELLO SANZIO (Urbino, 1483-1520): *La Fornarina*. Oil on panel, 85 x 60 cm. Rome, Galleria Nazionale d'Arte Antica.

Plate 7. BERNARDINO LUINI (c. 1480-1532): *The Dispute with the Doctors* (detail). Fresco, Saronno Sanctuary.

The painter returned soon afterwards, probably because of his love for Lucrezia and for his city. He took part in the decoration of the Medici villa of Poggio a Cajano (1521) and the Cloister of the Chiesa dello Scalzo (1514-1517 and 1522-1526), and in 1525 he painted the *Madonna del Sacco* fresco in a lunette of the Great Cloister of the Annunziata Church in Florence, certainly one of his most memorable works.

When the Medici abandoned the city, Andrea's political support came to an end. At the end of the siege of Florence, he fell victim to the terrible plague which followed, ' without finding a remedy for his ill, and without caring much, his wife staying as far away as she could for fear of the plague, he died (they say) with hardly anyone noticing.'

It is clear that the alternatives facing Andrea del Sarto with the outbreak of the Mannerist styles—which were followed in Tuscany first by Beccafumi, Rosso and Pontormo, and then by Bronzino—created an understandable confusion in his life as well as in his work. It is obvious that he felt in sympathy with the formal pictorial requirements of the High Renaissance and that he endeavoured as far as possible to stand aside from the increasingly pressing problems arising from Mannerism, with its break-up of forms by chiaroscuro, as in Leonardo, which at best seems to envelop the figures, absorbing every physical detail. Colour emerges clearly and sharply from this darkness, painted almost in a *tachist* manner. It is then, as for example in the Scalzo *Visitation*, that Andrea del Sarto's work can be seen to relate directly with the restless art of the second half of the century, with its painters, such as Boscoli, aiming at a kind naturalistically inspired luminosity.

At other times, during the 1530's, which were so charged with tragedy for the life and political prestige of Florence, Andrea's colouring emerged from the very sharp, bright atmosphere, full of those pictorial values which seemed to look back to Florentine art of the fifteenth-century, to lead beyond Bronzino as far as Orazio Gentileschi, a century later. It seems likely that Andrea saw in the famous *Madonna del Sacco*, the sad rhythms which form one of the high peaks of Italian Mannerism. Avoiding fantastic exaggeration, he keeps a tight control on his own imagination while still producing a work of profound spiritual significance.

Such was the achievement of Andrea del Sarto, an artist who laid the foundations for figurative research which were to reappear constantly during the century. In the work reproduced here, we can see how the artists of the second half of the century must have found in his exciting theme a fore-taste in dramatic invention, worthy to be placed alongside the achievements of Pontormo or Bronzino.

Plate 9—JACOPO DA PONTORMO: Visitation. The period at which the beautiful *Visitation* in the Pieve of Carmignano, was painted, is of exceptional interest in the life of Pontormo and the development of Italian Mannerism. This large panel was certainly painted before 1530, and in style follows that more physical and naturalistic expression of internal drama which moves from the Santa Felicita altarpiece to find complete expression in the *Supper at Emmaus* of Caravaggio.

Pontormo's profound, solitary melancholy, ready to break out in outbursts of a Saturnine humour, was certainly affected by Michelangelo during these years. But the conflict in Pontormo's style was more urgent and violent than in Michelangelo. Pontormo faced problems in Florence, in the midst of Mannerism, more demanding, vast and urgent

Plate 8. ANDREA DEL SARTO (Florence, 1486-1531):
The Sacrifice of Abraham. Panel, 98 x 69 cm. Madrid, Prado.

than did Rosso, with his morality, or Bronzino, with his illusory, paradoxical lucidity. From the frescoes in the Carthusian Monastery of Galluzzo to the *Deposition* in the Capponi Chapel in Santa Felicita, from the extraordinary decoration in Poggio a Cajano up to the deeply revealing drawings of his hypochondriacal old age, his career was almost an exception within the context of Tuscan art. His depth of feeling seems to have made him immune from the fissures with which time had shattered the structure of the Renaissance.

Compared with the surprisingly poor frescoes in the Carthusian Monastery, which foreshadow the Counter Reformation, the decorations in the Villa of Poggio a Cajano, or even the Carmignano *Visitation*, have a happy naturalism, as mellow as ripe fruit: their dramatic infusion of light and passionate humanity have caused many people to speak of Pontormo as a prophet of Caravaggio.

Pontormo is without doubt the most complex character in the profoundly intellectual phenomenon of Mannerism: it is impossible to sum him up in a few words. At first a pupil of Piero di Cosimo, he seemed to take to their farthest lengths the consequences of manneristic theory, accepting—at the time of the Carthusian Monastery frescoes—the suggestion of Dürer and northern influences. As he matured he seemed, at least externally, to enter into competition with Michelangelo suggesting an argument with him which did not escape his contemporaries. Their hostile attitude may be summed up in that of Cellini, who, working towards a formal return to classicism saw his work dangerously disruptive elements.

In order to understand this highly important moment in Pontormo's development, we ought to possess the frescoes in the Church of San Lorenzo in Florence. They were begun in 1546 and were his occupation until his death, twenty years later, but are now completely destroyed. The artist's old age is sombrely echoed in the laconic notes to his diary, richly illustrated with the most beautiful drawings, and which still exists today. During the long years which led up to his death, Pontormo withdrew from the world, as if fearful of the quarrel he had made with Michelangelo's titanic vision, and the spectral dissolution of form which he anticipated.

Plate 10—ROSSO FIORENTINO: Deposition. This great composition, one of the masterpieces of Florentine Manneristic painting, seems to derive from the fifteenth-century. And it must be said that the reasons for this neo-archaic inspiration certainly go beyond mere chance, and are of vital importance if this period and stylistic moment in the artist's life are to be understood. He became more and more inclined to abstraction, searching for a direct link between an abbreviated and immediate rendering of form and an absolutely 'abstract' colour. This intellectual duality is the basis of his entire work.

In this work Rosso Fiorentino seems to aspire to an intellectual purity, which enabled a cold dynamism to develop out of his 'manner'. There was, so to speak, an irrational participation in the life of painting as traditionally envisaged; and it represented a dissociation from those elements which the Renaissance had firmly held together, not only in its theoretical writings but especially in the personalities of its artists. This attitude which we have called purism had more than one similarity with the political life of Florence in those difficult years between the fall of the Republic and the start of the painstaking restoration of Cosimo I. It was echoed too, during the same years, in the Dürer-

like inspiration of Pontormo's frescoes in the Carthusian Monastery and the neo-archaic tone in the first efforts of Bronzino, his pupil.

However, within the purity which these artists searched for, the most committed Manneristic concepts can be discovered. Within the vast movement of Mannerism, which was born in Florence and found its archetype in the famous *Tondo Doni* of Michelangelo, the tormented figure of Rosso Fiorentino appears from the beginning as a character possessing a tragic yet coherent dignity, working in a decidedly anti-classical manner which constitutes a fundamental element in the intellectual revolt against the Apollonian certainty of the Renaissance world.

An unearthly light floods this cool, rational composition shining on the great figures, the solemn drapery, and the dramatic gestures, transfixed in time. The participants in this cerebral drama stand motionless in a glow that transforms their story.

Rosso was first a follower of Andrea del Sarto; then in Rome in 1524 he became an admirer of Michelangelo. He was active in Perugia, Florence and Venice, and was then invited to the court of Francis I, where he remained until his death. His presence in France was a determining factor in the development of the Renaissance outside Italy, and his influence may be seen in the admirable decoration of the great palace of Fontainebleau.

Plate 11—AGNOLO BRONZINO: Portrait of Guidubaldo di Montefeltro. Bronzino's art, represented here by a youthful work, the *Portrait of Guidubaldo di Montefeltro*, is by its very nature difficult to understand, not only because of the complexity of the themes, but also because of the complex culture, from which he seems to derive his inspiration.

First and foremost it is intimately related to the decline of Renaissance ideals, and to the irrevocable progress of the Counter-Reformation, which was initiated in Florence by Cosimo I de' Medici.

It does not seem possible to fix the stages of the artist's evolution and the decisive changes in his development. From around 1530—the date of the painting reproduced here—until at least 1550, that is, from the years of his early maturity until he was on the threshold of a profound crisis, Bronzino displayed a cold, almost glacial image of a world of inverted intellectuality. His best works seem to be a defence put up against the problems of his time.

The sharp composition, like an heraldic device, defines an architectonic and geometric space. The figure is placed in such a way that it gives rise to few problems of scale. We have here a simple condensation of spatial problems, offered to the light with the cold certainty of an artist skilful in solving formal and pictorial problems. Everything is clarity and brightness, within an apparently simple composition. Yet within the space of the perspective, a silence, imperceptible yet ever-present, vibrates on the hard and metallic surfaces. That indestructible element of the great Florentine tradition, the line, is reborn again, clinging to the choicest materials, bright and hard as a diamond.

Bronzino's art is best regarded as a constant exercise in metaphor, even if this is concealed under a veil of apparent simplicity. The metaphor conditions the choice of the means of expression. Behind this defense lies a genuine personality, and in this connection the verses composed by Bronzino are particularly revealing, for they speak perhaps more sincerely than his paintings do of his feelings of anxiety, and of the subtle precautions which defend his indolence.

Plate 10. ROSSO FIORENTINO (Florence, 1495-1550): *Deposition*. Oil on panel, 196 x 333 cm. Signed and dated 1521. Volterra Museum.

Plate 11. AGNOLO BRONZINO (Florence, 1503-1572): *Portrait of Guidubaldo di Montefeltro.* Oil on panel, 114 x 68 cm. Florence, Pitti Palace.

All the greatest portraits produced during the twenty years between 1530 and 1550, and after, contain traces of this spiritual and moral extroversion, as if the artist renounced his own personality and transferred it to his painting. The greatest and most successful example of this identification can be seen in the frescoes in the Chapel of Eleonora of Toledo in the Palazzo Vecchio. Here the 'transfer' is complete, and it represents Bronzino's highest achievement. The cold, but often sublime, voice of his poetry transforms the formal grandeur of the high Tuscan tradition. The product of this highly individual 'manner' is an almost surrealist enchantment, outside time.

Plate 12—ANTONIO ALLEGRI, called CORREGGIO: Two Putti (*detail*). This great artist's date of birth is enveloped in complete mystery, and in spite of vast amount of research which has been made into the subject, Correggio's artistic education remains even more mysterious. The possibility that he depended only on local influences may be discounted immediately, for such an exceptional art could have come into being only through an apprenticeship in a great centre of civilisation. Correggio must therefore have spent his youth in the Mantuan court of the Gonzagas and have been a pupil of Andrea Mantegna, whose long and important life had just ended at the start of the new century.

The young artist was mentioned in reliable records as having worked on the completion of the decoration of the 'Mantegna' Chapel, in the Church of St. Andrea. There may be speculation concerning that particular problem now, but there can be no doubt that the large rondels painted in fresco in the church, although a little later, relate the artist to the last period of Mantegna's activity.

Among these frescoes is the wonderful *Deposition*.

Mantegna's city and painting were, however, merely a point of reference to Correggio. Yet the whole art of the north revolved around Mantegna, from the precociously classical art of the Ferrarese artist Costa, to the burning colour of the works of Dosso Dossi. The disquieting shade of Leonardo, hanging over Milan and the tepid naturalism of Lombard painting, which showed all the intellectual doubt and unresolved difficulties of its own inventor, seems to find its real fulfilment in the human, sensual warmth of Correggio, who soon achieved a greater breadth of spirit.

After some paintings attributed to him at a fairly early date, he painted the *Madonna of St. Francis* (now in Dresden) between 1514 and 1515. Then a few years later, in 1518, he painted his first absolute masterpiece, the decoration of the Prioress's Room in the Parma Convent of St Paul. This work underwent a curious fate: unknown even to the most staunch supporters of Correggio in the seventeenth century, it was rediscovered by Ireneo Affò at the end of the eighteenth. Correggio represented the allegorical aspects of hunting. He was encouraged by the donor, Donna Giovanna da Piacenza, and the many cultured people who were to be found at that flourishing court. The composition is placed within a false vine trellis, draped over sixteen sections of the ceiling, where among branches and festoons of fruit, tender putti rise above the illusory roof of greenery, at the base of which sixteen lunettes glitter like monochrome cameos, each representing a mythological subject.

Correggio had already reached full maturity and appeared the most advanced of all the century's artists both in style and expression. His line was not suppressed or overpowered by the famous chiaroscuro of Leonardo's

Lombard followers, but was alive and gently palpitating, tracing new variations of perspective which no longer bore any relation to the fifteenth century geometric scheme or to the rigorously pyramidal construction of Roman classical compositions. The whole work is bathed in atmospheric light, and to complete this marvellous 'plein air' a new feeling for colour appears. A gentle classicism appears to be born anew through some subtle dialogue or mysterious conversation, and an almost direct communication leads from it to the neo-Classical age, at the end of the eighteenth century.

Plate 13—ANTONIO ALLEGRI called CORREGGIO: The Madonna of St Jerome.

This famous painting was produced at the same time as the work on the cupola of Parma Cathedral. It was formerly in the Church of St Anthony and is now in Parma's National Gallery. This work has always been a great source of controversy to art critics, from Vasari, who expressed deep admiration for it, by way of Algarotti in the eighteenth century, who sums up most of the opinions as follows: 'May the divine genius of Raphael forgive me, if on looking at this painting I have broken faith with him, and have been tempted to say to Correggio in secret: you alone please me!'

During the years after the death of Raphael and the completion of the Sistine Chapel, it was Correggio who represented the highest achievements of Italian art. It has never been confirmed by his biographers that he went to Rome before he began to work on the Cupola of the Church of St John the Evangelist, but it is very difficult to believe that the thorough knowledge of the Roman works of the two greatest artists known which he showed in his work could have come to him only by means of drawings or engravings. It is now generally believed that Correggio must have visited Rome and seen the works there. Yet Correggio, especially in the two cupolas in Parma, goes beyond these limits and moves right to the frontiers of the Baroque.

The force which spirals through the great cupola of the Cathedral, a dream of gentle sensuality, full of light, full of secret intimacy and abandon. Its boldness of perspective and foreshortening inspired many later painters. Admiration has been almost unanimous in every century, from Titian onwards, who declared his astonishment to one of the churchwardens who was bold enough to declare it 'a frogs' pool'. According to tradition, this expression so embittered the artist that he abandoned his work and retired to solitude in Correggio, and even if this tradition is false, it does indicate the Church's attitude, at a time when the Counter-Reformation was preparing for this joy in the flesh, permeated, and given form by the pagan flood of light.

The *Madonna of St Jerome*, known as 'Day', together with the other famous Madonnas, '*Madonna of the Porringer*' and '*Night*', bring to an end Correggio's activity at the same time as the Cathedral cupola. St Jerome and the gentle Magdalen are the pivots of the composition, and in the space between their bodies the vision of the Virgin and Child appears. The formal and emotional perfection of this painting was fully appreciated in Correggio's own day, and has come down to us in no way diminished. It is the light which is most striking, the warm, golden, supernal light. It created legends about the technique which was employed, brushwork in gold, it was said; and caused the Bavarian painter and critic, Anthony Raphael Mengs, the most subtle of Correggio's admirers, to write '... the colours seem not to be applied by the brush, but are as if melted together in the manner of wax over a fire '.

Plate 14—FRANCESCO MAZZOLA called PARMIGIANINO : Madonna dal Collo Lungo (long-necked Madonna). The artist was commissioned to execute this painting in 1534 by Elena Baiardi, the wife of Francesco Tagliaferri, and was paid for the work in advance. Was to be completed by the following Whitsun, that is, in 1535 : but it remained unfinished, as the little inscription on the column to the right shows. Its state was respected by the donor, and placed in the Baiardi Chapel in the Church of the Servi in Parma after Parmigianino's death, that is, in 1542. At the end of the seventeenth century it was sold by the monks, not without some opposition from the family of the donor, to Ferdinando de' Medici, Grand Duke of Tuscany, and is now in the Uffizi Gallery in Florence.

There are few works which answer so clearly to the modern definition of ' Mannerism '. It represents one of the most pagan episodes in the whole history of Italian art. The inspiration is elegant worldliness, of an intimately intellectual subtlety, its rhythms are of an almost oriental beauty. The perfect measure of the column in the background marks the proportion and formal arrangement of the painting, from the ' long ' neck of the Virgin to the almost Egyptian head of the babe, and the perfect, tapered legs of the angel who encloses the painting on the left. A worldly interpretation has been given to the sacred event, and a superb hedonism emerges from the gentle fixed gaze of the participants; while beneath the silken robes barely draped over the beautiful hermaphroditic figures, a quivering sensuality hides. A silvery sheen pervades the painting, gathering reflections from the surfaces of cool flesh. Mannerism was a current of Renaissance thought which emerged at the very beginning of the sixteenth century. It found a new means of expression for the deepest and most

secret doubts and animosities which arose from the difficulty—at first only perceived, but then present in a more and more dramatic form—of attaining the absolute perfection of the classical ideal. It was thus far from representing an evolution of classical thought, for it soon became revealed as the antithesis of this concept, even when, as in the case of Bronzino, the apparent and external form appears to contain all the perfect virtues in a general equilibrium of form and content. This crisis, which was echoed in so many ways in the political and social life of the time, was to carry away even those which seemed most strongly aware of the closed ambit of classical culture. If Michelangelo had already shown awareness of this problem, and then continuously took up the theme throughout his life of titanic struggles, Raphael himself—a few years before his premature death—was inclining towards the desire to wander beyond the confines of perfection, on to the vast field of intellectualism. From Tuscany the earliest and most anxious voices answered this inner discord, dramatically expressed by Beccafumi, Rosso, Pontormo and Anselmi, who owed a great deal to Parmigianino, the greatest exponent of northern Mannerism.

Plate 15—FRANCESCO MAZZOLA called PARMIGIANINO: The Santa Margherita Madonna. This panel was painted for the Church of Santa Margherita in Bologna in 1529. It echoes in a strangely different manner the *Madonna of St Jerome* which Correggio, an artist of so different a temperament, was at that same time painting for the altar of the Church of St Antony in Parma. The comparison is valuable, for it reveals that the basis of Mannerism was not only a matter of psychological attitude, but of theory as well. This can be seen from a comparison of the

style of Correggio's great work with Parmigianino's manner in imitating it. That diffused, and pleasing grandeur, that delicate light which spreads over the figures, forming the features of a gentle and classically composed humanity, are replaced here by a humid and shadowy tone which appears to emerge from beneath. The light rays seem to penetrate the coverlet of dark green, and the figures are bathed in light. Parmigianino's is an essentially Romantic painting, one of the most celebrated of his works, and in it the mental oppression typical of Mannerism is expressed, it might be said in terms of Nature and plant life. The feet are planted on the ground like the roots of trees, the folds of drapery recall the living bark of trees. If the subject of Correggio's great picture was that of light—it was indeed called 'The Day', so the work of Parmigianino might be termed if not 'Night' then 'Shadow,' so mysterious and veiled is it in feeling.

This painting was mentioned in some deeds in 1529, which record that it was bought from a certain Giovanni Maria Giusti for the family chapel in the Church of Santa Margherita in Bologna.

The principal events of the age of Mannerism in north Italy did not come to an end with Parmigianino. In Bologna in particular, perhaps owing to an anti-classical element in the history of the city (to be understood, however, as chiefly anti-Roman), there was no lack of great and important artists. We need but recall Primaticcio, who worked in Fontainebleau with Rosso Fiorentino, where he planted the seeds of that special love for classical elegy which became a fundamental theme of French painting. Niccolò dell'Abate of Modena was another painter who went to Paris; in the Poggi Palace in Bologna some outstanding works of his are to be seen. They are like a colourful, imaginative and humorous epilogue to the chivalrous culture going back to the poet Ariosto and the painter Dosso Dossi. In Bologna, too, there is the important work of Pellegrino Tibaldi, in which the imitation of Michelangelo is subject to a distinctly " Lombard " flavour, thus preparing the ground for Lodovico, Agostino and Annibale Carracci. Another, but more isolated deviation from the Michelangelo style is found in the work of the Ferrarese artist Sebastiano Fillippi, known as Bastianino, forceful and full of foretastes of Romanticism.

Plate 16—LODOVICO CARRACCI: St John the Baptist Preaching. This is one of the greatest and most important paintings in the entire output of Lodovico Carracci and of the school of Bologna. It was at one time in the church of the Carthusian Monastery, facing the equally famous *Communion of St Jerome* by Agostino Carracci. The seventeenth-century historian C. C. Malvasia commented on this evidently intentional rivalry, and his words can hardly be bettered: 'Thus to that picture, which is a harmonious blend of all the styles, is contrasted this one in a single manner, but in that of the greatest painter of the Venetian school, if not of the whole world. Everything is changed into Paolo (Veronese); and where the St Jerome appears to have been finished with great feeling, one admires his (Lodovico Carracci's) St John for being done almost casually: just enough colours and no more: not all that excessive working, these repeats and revisions; it is made to flow from the brush with consummate ease, as if by chance, here and there with studied carelessness, the ground being sometimes allowed to provide the shadow. The grandeur and shaggy majesty of the main figure and the movement of the others have no equal.'

It now seems certain, after the many years during which the contrary view held tradi-

Plate 14. FRANCESCO MAZZOLA called PARMIGIANINO (Parma, 1503-1540):
Madonna dal Collo Lungo. Oil on panel, 216 x 132 cm. Florence, Uffizi.

tional sway, that a really up-to-date evaluation of the work of the older Carracci must place him in his rightful position as the creator and father of local painting, through two centuries and on to the twenty years of the Baroque. From his powerful and complex character diverse and apparently contrasting attitudes emerge: and this contradiction is very obvious in Lodovico, only being resolved in the passionate preoccupation with his work. These diverse attitudes have inspired new painters from time to time, who were destined to create history in Bologna in future years. The first of these painters, Guido Reni and Albani, soon left their native city but were close followers of Lodovico at the end of the century. Of the second generation, we need only mention the more modest, but very important, Tiarini, Mastelletta, Cavedone, Massari, Brizio, Garbieri... In addition some of the characteristics of the most grandiloquent Baroque period, which apparently owed their origin to his cousin Annibale's greater pictorial virtuosity, were already to be found here, even if less perfected.

A Lombard painter, in the widest sense of the word, at a time when Lombardy included the entire Po Valley, Lodovico encompassed within a slow and at times laborious temperament the great moral anxiety aroused by the Council of Trent, meditating on matters of conscience, with the arrogance of the early Baroque style. And if at times within his vast compositions the tension slackens and notes of irony, rhetoric, even awkwardness, appear, his most secret inspiration can touch chords which vibrate with mystery and passion.

Plate 17—MICHELANGELO MERISI called CARAVAGGIO: Bacchus. The painter Baglione, who is the greatest of Caravaggio's historians, recalls that this is the first painting executed by Caravaggio after his stay in the studio of the Cavalier d'Arpino: '...and the first was a Bacchus with some bunches of grapes, made with great diligence'. On the basis of this testimony, rather than of its style, it is believed that this work must have been painted around 1589.

With this painting, which is apparently so subtle and calm, the reservations of Mannerism disappear, while for the first time in the history of art the work of the painter is no longer dedicated to the exigencies of commissions and content, but to a personal aim of pure naturalistic representation. Man and his conscience have become the only criteria in a long and solitary study. In Caravaggio's first works, the gypsy girl is represented in a pose as ancient as her poverty, a youth shudders at the bite of a lizard, or else is surprised among flowers and fruit in a tranquil setting; a family stops to rest in the evening in a landscape sweet with memories.

Caravaggio left Lombardy for Rome when he was a young man. He was born in 1573, and was little over ten years old when he entered Peterzano's studio, where he was to remain until the end of the 1580s. Michelangelo arrived in Rome between 1588 and 1589, and from that date began the main events in Caravaggio's life, so beloved of romantic biographers. After his apprenticeship, which lasted a few months, in the studio of the Cavalier d'Arpino, a wound caused him to be confined in the Hospital of the Consolation. To this period of his activity, closely related to Lombard painting, but already in a completely new atmosphere, belong the *Young Bacchus* in the Borghese Gallery, the *Flight into Egypt* in the Doria Gallery, the *Child Bitten by a Lizard* in the Longhi Collection, and the other famous works which place Caravaggio right at the

centre of a new movement. From then on his fame began to increase. In 1597 he was already mentioned as being famous. He became more and more involved in the murkiest episodes of artistic Bohemia in the Rome of those years. In this connection, the Dutch writer Van Mander made the well-known observation: 'He also has the fault that he does not wait quietly in his studio; when he has worked for two weeks, he takes a holiday for a month. With a sword at his side and a page following he passes from one prank to another, always ready to provoke and wrangle...' However, before the end of the century, the young painter's promise was wonderfully fulfilled. Of this period are works like the *Medusa* in the Uffizi, *Love the Conqueror* in Berlin, *St Francis in Ecstasy* in Hertford and *St John the Baptist* in the National Gallery of Rome: as well as the *Stories in the Life of St Matthew* which decorate the Contarelli Chapel of San Luigi dei Francesi. It is characteristic of Caravaggio that, faced with a task of decoration, he should abandon the technique of fresco and use instead the large canvas. This was typical of the Lombard tradition, and it allowed him to give greater animation to those theatrically violent gestures. These masterpieces remained in the artist's studio for a long time, and became the basis for the new Caravaggesque manner.

After the decidedly experimental period of the *Stories of St Matthew*, he appeared to be driven by a new consciousness of himself towards masterpieces like the *Martyrdom of St Peter* and the *Conversion of St Paul*, which were painted in 1601 for the Cerasi Chapel in the Church of Santa Maria del Popolo. In these paintings it is as if, having reached the climax of a drama, the cathartic moment becomes concrete in terms of painting, thus opening radically new paths to figurative art.

Plate 18—MICHELANGELO MERISI called CARAVAGGIO: The Supper at Emmaus.
Every phase of Caravaggio's painting had a great number of imitators who, at least for the first thirty years of the century, carried its message to every part of Europe. Indeed, as early as 1600, Rome appeared as a mirage to all the artists of Europe. With its palaces, its churches, its early collections, Rome was the great teacher during those years, in which art was the main topic of conversation and every point of view was discussed. Here were the naturalists who modelled themselves on Caravaggio, the classicists who chose as their model the Bolognese Annibale Carracci, and the last Mannerists, who in some ways continued in the old teachings of the preceding century. Already at the start of the century, Caravaggio had a large number of followers and friends, such as the German Elsheimer, Peter Paul Rubens and the Pisan Orazio Gentileschi. Even Orazio Borgianni, after a stay in Spain, was to paint in a way which had already been foreshadowed by the best Manneristic painting. While Gentileschi remained closely bound to the early naturalistic manner of Caravaggio, as to that which most closely related him to his own Florentine tradition, Borgianni developed his gifts of greater expressiveness, in a rich and modern vein. The Venetian Saraceni also remembered his own origins in the delicate colours of his paintings so that he returned in his old age to reminiscences of the sixteenth century. The imitation of Caravaggio followed a different course in Bartolomeo Manfredi, who was, however, a friend and ambassador of this new painting, in company with foreign artists like the Dutch Ter Brugghen, Gerrit Honthorst, Dirk Baburen, and the French Valentin and Simon Vouet. So, too, many Italians who were in Rome during those years, brought back to their native provinces fresh and original variants of Caravaggesque naturalism, among them

Plate 16. LODOVICO CARRACCI (Bologna, 1555-1619):
St John the Baptist Preaching. Oil on canvas, 380 x 227 cm.
Signed and dated MDICII Lud. Carrat. Fe. Bologna, National Gallery.

Plate 17. MICHELANGELO MERISI called CARAVAGGIO (Caravaggio, 1573-Rome, 1610):
Bacchus. Oil on canvas, 95 x 85 cm. Florence, Uffizi.

the Veronese artists Bassetti and Turchi, the Piedmontese Tanzio of Varallo, Nicolò Musso and Giuseppe Vermiglio, the Tuscans Grammatica, Riminaldi, Manetti and Rustici, the Genoese Fiasella, and that great genius Giovan Battista Caracciolo, called Battistello, who may be regarded as the most advanced Neapolitan painter of the seventeenth century. The artist Giovanni Serodine was very important as a purveyor of 'the Caravaggesque manner', and in his brief but outstanding career he continued the Caravaggesque tradition, attaining highly individual results.

Caravaggio's followers enjoyed full freedom of treatment and subject. The modern idea of still life was born of this freedom, as was the 'genre' painting of narrative and anecdote by the Bamboccianti which developed into a popular series of stories—a final and not unworthy version of Caravaggesque naturalism. Among artists who dedicated themselves to genre painting was Pieter Van Laer, a native of Haarlem, who during the thirteen years he worked in Rome laid the foundations for that chapter of Dutch art history from which, in diverse ways, were to be born the greatest painters of that country from De Hooch to Vermeer of Delft. Other Italian genre painters were Michelangelo Cerquozzi and Angeluccio, a pupil of Claude Lorrain.

Plate 19—MICHELANGELO MERISI called CARAVAGGIO: The Madonna and Child with St Anne, known as the Palafrenieri Madonna. According to contemporary biographers, this large altarpiece was painted for the altar of the Palafrenieri in St Peter's Basilica, Rome. It was later removed from the altar at the wish of the ecclesiastical authorities, and came into the possession of Cardinal Scipio Borghese.

This is a work of great monumentality, similar to the *Pellegrini Madonna* in the Church of St Agostino, the *Deposition of Christ* in the Vatican Gallery, and the *Death of the Virgin*, painted for the monks of Santa Maria della Scala and then refused because they considered it indelicate. Within the rhythmical composition, done for once in the classical manner, we can perceive the force of a drama bursting the bounds of a morality which had hitherto contained it. From this time too the artist's destiny rapidly took a tragic turn. Forced to leave Rome after a murder, he reached Naples where he produced within a short time, some of his greatest works such as the *Seven Works of Charity* for the Pio Monte and the *Madonna of the Rosery*, now in the Vienna Museum. These works are all of great narrative breadth, sustained by a continuous tension which appeared to foretell the tragic course of events. At the end of 1607, Caravaggio went to Malta and entered the service of the Grand Master of the Order. He painted some pictures, like the great *Beheading of the Baptist* for the Church of St John, in which more than one indication points to autobiography. The artist was involved in a further battle in the ensuing years, and had to flee from Malta. He was followed by hired assassins, and his life became fraught with danger; yet new works appeared, in Syracuse, Messina and Palermo. He was recognised by his pursuers in Naples at the door of an inn, and was wounded and disfigured. He loaded his few poor belongings on to a felucca, and in this state arrived in Porto Ercole, where, owing to a case of mistaken identity, he was imprisoned by the Spanish police. When released, he had lost his few belongings. Deprived of everything, and contracting an illness in the vast wastes of the countryside he made his way on foot to Rome. An attack of fever killed him on the journey.

This was on the 18th July, 1610. The news reached Rome on the 28th, and three days later the Papal chancery, by a cruel irony, announced the remission of the proclamation which had condemned Caravaggio to exile.

After his flight from Rome, when he was staying in Malta, and still more so during his anxious peregrinations through Sicily, his work show a new and tortured relationship between figures and space, with a mysterious and monumental quality leading to the climax of that dramatic tension which is peculiar him. This appears in the *Beheading of St John* painted for Malta Cathedral—a sublime representation of a tragic and fearful event. A heightened sense of drama marks too the Sicilian altarpieces, which are of pallid colour and tortured forms; *The Resurrection of Lazarus*, and the *Adoration of the Shepherds* (both in Messina), the *Burial of St Lucia* (in Syracuse), and the *Nativity with St Lorenzo and St Francis* (in Palermo).

With the sudden death of Caravaggio, the legacy of his style and humanity passed to his imitators. Not only the last painter of the Renaissance, he should be considered as the first great artist of the modern age. His message was intentionally human and easily understood. His work contains the seeds of an artistic revolution, on the fruit of which we are still living.

Plate 20—GUIDO RENI: The Massacre of the Innocents. Of all the works which make up the vast catalogue of Guido Reni's oeuvre this is perhaps the most famous; and, for once at least, it must be admitted that popular judgment coincides with expert evaluation. It was conceived and executed when the artist was still a young man (he was just past forty) and clearly shows the evidence of his recent experiments, during the ten years which

he had spent largely in Rome. His biographers and historians, supported by documentary evidence, believe the painting to have been executed after a sudden break in his stay at Rome, and before he began his work of decorating the Paolina Chapel in the church of Santa Maria Maggiore, which was to be his first occupation as soon as he returned to the capital a year later. It seems too that Guido had undertaken to do this painting a few years previously for the Berò family who wished to have it placed in the church of San Domenico in Bologna.

This painting was produced at the precise moment when, after his sudden return to Bologna, Guido Reni encountered the most compelling ideas of the classical conception of art, and his work was to remain typical of those artists who followed this tendency. It was a few months since the generous and ' heroic ' Annibale Carracci had died, and his works were making an ever-greater impact on the feeling of the time as well as on the personality of Guido Reni. The way led to a glorious future: to Poussin, Lorrain and Dughet, and to Albani and Domenichino. During the last years of his life, Annibale Carracci suffered from an illness which finally killed him. He had continually strived for an intellectual rendering of the classical theme, varying his inspiration from the lyricism of figures and landscape to an elaborate composition of sacred and mythological scenes. The Farnese Gallery was destined to become a living repository of the old way of painting and the new, with its febrile naturalism within a a formal, classical frame.

His colourful vision was to become dear to the painters of the great Roman Baroque. At times it expressed a theoretical neo-classicism, while at others he was already of the Romantic school. Guido Reni was an outstanding personality, violently egocentric but secretly tormented. It appeared that he

Plate 18. MICHELANGELO MERISI, called CARAVAGGIO (Caravaggio, 1573-Rome 1610):
The Supper at Emmaus. Oil on canvas 139 x 195 cm. London, National Gallery.

Plate 19. MICHELANGELO MERISI called CARAVAGGIO (Caravaggio, 1573-Rome 1610):
The Madonna and Child with St Anne, known as the *Palafrenieri Madonna*.
Oil on canvas, 292 x 211 cm. Rome, Borghese Gallery.

was almost distrustful of contemporary painting, and was prepared to return, as he did in his old age, to the Mannerism of the Counter-Reformation.

'What I paint are the ideal forms which are fixed forever in my mind' the artist is said to have declared: and no clearer declaration of a stylistic conscience has ever been made, even if it was said in similar words by Raphael more than a century before. This supreme idealisation, which was Guido Reni's driving force, is to be seen in the strictly classical attitude of the *Massacre of the Innocents*, where every gesture is linked together in a subtle rhythmic composition; with the horror tempered by dignity, and the violence in a terrified cry.

Plate 21—GUIDO RENI: Salomé with the Head of the Baptist. After his great successes in Rome in the first twenty years of the century, Guido Reni returned to Bologna and worked there until his death in 1632. His last paintings show a constant idealisation of form, embracing in a pure atmosphere the most discordant and clamorous elements of the Baroque.

His story, told by that invigorating art critic Canon Malvasia, is very revealing. He was a man of suspicious fears, secrets and enormous egotism, and appeared to direct his whole energy towards a purposeful purification of pictorial ideas and the means of expression relating to them: as if to produce an exceptional and splendid 'metaphysic of costume', analogous in intent, if not in style, to the art of the French Jansenist Philippe de Champaigne. But in Guido Reni the idealism remains untouched and uncorrupted to the end, although its tenderness gently anticipates the art of the Romantic period.

In this painting, which represents a subject treated many times by Guido Reni, *Salomé*

with the head of the Baptist, which was mentioned in the eighteenth century as being in the Palazzo Corsini in Rome and is still in that collection as part of the State collections, the artist who has now grown old is still developing with as much intensity as ever. On the basis of documentation as well as style, it is agreed that this painting must have been executed a little after 1630. It is from this year that, having made an unsuccessful attempt at a neo-Venetian colouring, such as can be seen in the Louvre *Rape of Helen*, Guido Reni seemed to withdraw into a private world, peopled by phantoms. The colours merge into subtle and evanescent tones. Guido's previous preoccupation with the classical ideal (see the preceding plate, *Massacre of the Innocents*), has gone, and his modelling has lost its certainty, its texture, and its outline, becoming marked by more and more rapid brush strokes, light strokes following dark, achieving a sort of neo-classical Impressionism. These works of Guido Reni, and still more so the later ones, have given rise to the criticism that his works are 'unfinished', and to the legends of his negligence because he was weighed down by debt. In fact, even if this work really does seem to be unfinished, left uncompleted in the artist's studio, his last works show that he was freeing himself from every external factor which he considered to be impeding him, so that he might express freely in his work the eternal, celestial vision of the truth. In this we see the last survival of the rigours of the Counter-Reformation, at the time of the triumph of Baroque.

Plate 22—DOMENICO ZAMPIERI called DOMENICHINO: The Martyrdom of St Peter. We know from the Roman historian Bellori, who followed the events connected with the new passion for classicism in seventeenth-century Rome, that this large canvas was commissioned from Domenichino by the Marquis G. Filippo Spada for the Dominican Convent of Brisighella. It was removed to France by Napoleon's forces, and returned to Italy after the Restoration; it is now in the Bologna National Gallery.

This is one of the few works which Domenichino, who was Bolognese by birth and education, left in his birthplace. It was painted during the short time he stayed in Bologna between 1617 and 1621, before returning finally to Rome and Naples. In the frescoes in the Abbey of Grottaferrata, and then in the amazing decoration in the Chapel of St Cecilia in the church of San Luigi dei Francesi in Rome (1615-17), Domenichino had acquired a vigour which was to inspire many great artists who strove to depict in a similar way their vision of Arcady: a vision in which imagination had full rein, and was not chilled by classical concepts. This attitude—which in *The Martyrdom of St Peter* moved away in a decidely more naturalistic direction—was particularly widespread in Rome through the Farnese Gallery and the last works of Annibale Carracci. A feeling of constant melancholy pervaded art, a nostalgia for an age finally lost to man. This feeling was particularly noticeable, first through direct collaboration and then through a reminiscence of style, in Domenichino himself, then in the Bolognese Albani, in whom a more Romantic element appeared, with neo-Venetian colour, and finally in the French artists Claude Lorrain, Gaspard Dughet, and the ultimate master of European classicism, Nicolas Poussin. Around these artists were others whose work occasionally showed similar elements, artists such as Bril and Tassi, Cozza and Sassoferrato, Andrea Sacchi and Pietro da Cortona (who was to become the principal exponent of Roman Baroque).

Meanwhile in Bologna, at the end of the 1620s, young artists were still being inspired by the teaching of Lodovico Carracci and the painters of the oldest 'Lombard' tradition. There lived Guido Reni; and it was he who, on the death of Lodovico in 1619, assumed the moral supremacy which was to lead him, almost in isolation, to dominate Bolognese painting.

This firm supremacy vanquished all the imitators of Lodovico Carracci, who had been of great importance at the beginning of the century: artists such as Mastelletta, Cavedobe and Tiarini. With Guercino isolated in his final manner, there was nothing to be done but to wait for the mid-century to bring the renewal of painting through the works of, first, Simone Cantarini, then Pasinelli, Cignani and Canuti, with their historical linearity embracing a new Baroque feeling. Giuseppe Maria Crespi was forcibly struck by these artists when in the early eighteenth century he became one of the great naturalistic painters of Europe.

Plate 23—FRANCESCO SOLIMENA: Judith with the Head of Holophernes. The seventeenth century had opened in Naples with the lively presence of Caravaggio: and highly important and fascinating traces of his passage remain in the works of *San Domenico*, *Pio Monte* or *St Anne* in the Lombardi Church in Naples. The most important recipient of this revolutionary legacy was Battistello Caracciolo, whom we know as a naturalistic and intimate painter from the 1620s and who with the passage of years became more gentle and serene, as if returning to the problems which had occupied the sixteenth century. Other artists revolved around him, although they were inferior, such as Sellitto, Finoglia, and even Stanzione,

who was also interested in new variants on classical themes. The Spanish artist Jusepe Ribera was later to bring to the naturalistic art of Naples new themes, consisting in a Baroque distortion of feeling together with a strict observance of the laws of composition. Following after him were painters like Passante, Guarino, Giovanni Do or Fracanzano. Other artists were later to renew the glory of Neapolitan painting of the seventeenth century: Aniello Falcone and Bernardo Cavallino. The painter Cavallino had a more subtle and elegant forms and colour, and the works he produced towards the middle of the century were comparable to those of Guido Reni in Bologna.

But there was soon to burst upon Naples the neo-Venetian and Baroque style, which found its highest expression in Mattia Preti and Luca Giordano. The churches and palaces became filled with brilliant decorations, in rich and lively colouring, with hints of Romanticism. When Charles II sent for Luca Giordano to go to Spain in 1692, the new century had in a sense already begun, although this could be seen only in the nostalgic naturalism of Mattia Preti, who was still painting in the manner of the early seventeenth century.

The conditions of work which confronted Luca Giordano owed much to the superb achievements of Roman Baroque. The names which come most readily to mind are those of Lanfranco and especially Piero da Cortona, whose works enabled Giordano to place within an open and infinite perspective his rich and vital scenes, which form a wonderful compendium of Neapolitan seventeenth-century art. Popular tradition gave him the nickname of 'Luca fa presto' ('Luke the Hurried'), and his works soon became known throughout Europe, while his nickname reflects his incredible energy. This was to lead to the Spanish tradition of Goya which from the beginning of the eighteenth century became assimilated into the Neapolitan.

Neapolitan Baroque art flourished in the eighteenth century, and was rich and proud even of its minor characters, such as De Matteis, De Mura or Giacomo del Po, who travelled around Europe bringing with them the influence of Luca Giordano. But the greatest of all these eighteenth-century Neapolitan artists was Francesco Solimena. He studied painting at the height of the seventeenth century, and first continued the naturalistic tradition of Mattia Preti, with its violence and passion, although he purified this warm expressiveness with a greater control of form. Light enters the painting from every side, but instead of becoming dispersed in an joyful picturesqueness, as in Giordano, it becomes little by little a means of describing relationships, sometimes becoming slightly academic although without losing grandeur and dignity.

With the swan song of Baroque decoration in Corrado Giaquinto and the violent return to naturalism in Gaspare Traversi the period of Baroque painting in Naples comes to an end.

Even a brief outline of seventeenth-century Neapolitan painting cannot overlook that essential element in the history and life of the city, the 'still life', which continued far into the succeeding century. As we know, this 'genre' was born of the violent art of Caravaggio, and its fortune, especially in Rome, remained first within the hands of the artists of Caravaggio's close circle, and then broadened as it became welcomed by art lovers and collectors. We do not know the precise date of the origin of this 'genre' in Naples, but it is believed to have started in the works of modestly successful artists, like Giacomo Recco, Luca Forte and Ambrosiello Faro. Later, the celebrated painter of still lifes, Paolo Porpora introduced his flash of virtuoso

Plate 20. GUIDO RENI (Bologna, 1575-1642): *The Massacre of the Innocents*. Oil on canvas, 268 x 170 cm. Bologna, National Gallery.

Plate 21. GUIDO RENI (Bologna, 1575-1642): *Salomé with the Head of the Baptist*. Oil on canvas, 134 x 97 cm. Rome, National Gallery of Ancient Art.

brilliance into the tumult of Baroque, which was to meet with such success during the middle years of the century. G. B. Ruoppolo, who was influenced directly by Michelangelo Cerquozzi, follows in this direction. He was a pupil of Porpora, and was engaged in the problem of translating the taste for still life into a Baroque language. He solved this problem by painting in a Baroque manner while retaining definite traces of his naturalistic education. Another great artist of the Neapolitan still-life in the seventeenth century was Giuseppe Recco, who was a little younger than Ruoppolo. He followed a different direction from that of the artists already mentioned: for example, his work shows the influence of the Lombard still-life and a great debt to Flemish artists. He was not unaware either of the work of some Spanish artists. But the greatest and most personal work of Giuseppe Recco was without a doubt his great still-lifes of fish and sea creatures. These paintings are of staggeringly ' Baroque ' vitality, and have a truth to nature which obviously owes much to naturalistic origins.

From at least 1670 the Flemish artist Abraham Breughel was in Naples. He brought a more ornate and decorative art which had arisen in Rome with such painters as Mario dei Fiori. In the eighteenth century, the same tradition prevailed, producing the surprisingly delicate art of that delightful painter, Andrea Belvedere.

Plate 24—ALESSANDRO MAGNASCO: Penitent Friars.

Magnasco's work cannot be considered as purely Genoese. It has, in addition, certain harsher elements which derive from the tendencies inherent in the Counter-Reformation painting which were to strike him particularly during his stay in Milan. In Milan too, the dying memories of late Mannerism were to reach him from Carlo Borromeo, by way of Cerano, Morazzone, and Cairo, among others. His time in Milan was fruitful in that it allowed him to mingle with artists of other traditions, in particular with Sebastiano Ricci.

Ricci is a painter who has often been underrated. He has been accused of plagiarism (Corregio and Guercino) and of superficiality. In fact he forms an important link between the sixteenth century Venetian painters and the great final flourish of Giambattista Tiepolo. Ricci was a colourist in the grand tradition, and his frescoes and easel paintings show energy, independence, and an accomplished sense of composition. His influence on Magnasco is definite, and definitely instructive. The gay, lively Venetian manner lifted Magnasco, anyway for a time, out of his natural introspection and pessimism.

Magnasco's first works were portraits, painted under Abbiati in Milan. Unfortunately these have been lost to us. He is also known to have executed some large religious subjects, but our only evidence of these is his *Supper at Emmaus* in the Convent of St Francis, a very accomplished work. Milan was at this time under the domination of Spain, and an unpleassantly blinkered and avaricious atmosphere prevailed at the court of the Duke. The artist's bitterness and cynicism may well have been triggered off by this situation, but he dutifully produced painting for the Duchy in a suitable style, with subjects like *Don Quixote*.

The work which we think of today as Magnascesque was done during his ' third period ' between 1711 and 1735 in Milan and in Genoa between 1715 and 1749. Later Magnasco worked for a time for the Duke of Florence. He died in Genoa, old, tired, embittered, perhaps, by the meteoric success of Tiepolo.

Magnasco's name was forgotten after his death, and for many years his reputation lay in cold storage. Recently, however, he has re-emerged with an important place in the history of European painting. He is classed by some with Bosch, Goya and Daumier as one of the great satirists, on account of the genre paintings with the 'little figures' done between 1711 and 1749. These are very numerous and are the result of a strong compulsion to express in paint the bitter feelings which became even obsessions. The scenes repeat themselves many times and are mainly limited to scenes of brigandage, or rough soldiery, the tortures of the Inquisition, scenes with monks or nuns or prisons or grotesque masques. Like Goya he saw in the masked carnival something sinister, as if the disguises of men became the deformity of mankind itself. They are painted most minutely with tiny painstaking brush strokes, the figures dwarfed by the disproportionate surroundigs. Whereas in most genre painting the artist is extolling the simple, familiar scene, in Magnasco the penetration is deeper, the attitude different. . He seeks not to reflect on the intimacy but to draw conclusions from it—

conclusions which were often brutally cynical. As he grew older the calm surface of his work became more and more agitated, until, in his great old age his pictures became the teasing distortions of sheer tragedy, scarcely mitigated by the echoes of his sardonic laughter.

This applies to his best work, rightly famous. Other paintings fall short in some way, owing to a suspicion of slickness. He painted quickly, sometimes too quickly and his work suffered as a result. But there can be no doubt that Magnasco brought a new richness to late Italian Baroque, an extraordinary pictorial vivacity which had a parallel in the work of the Lombard Ceruti and the Bolognese Crespi. If he drew inspiration from the Venetians from the point of veiw of colour, he was overwhelmed by its explosiveness and floridness and turned away from it, fortunately for us, to produce works of an intimacy, profundity and independence which have gained him a justly high position.

Plate 23. FRANCESCO SOLIMENA (Naples, 1657-1747):
Judith with the Head of Holophernes. Oil on canvas, 316 x 432 cm.
Cornigliano (Genoa), Villa Bombrini.

Plate 24. ALESSANDRO MAGNASCO (Genoa, 1667-1749):
Penitent Friars. Florence, Pitti Palace.

School of
LOMBARDY

School of
EMILIA

School of
PADUA

School of
VENICE

SAVOY

School of
FERRARA

School of
PIEDMONT

School of
BOLOGNA

School of
FLORENCE

School of
SIENA

Turin

Milan

Brescia

Padua

Venice

Parma

Genoa

Modena

Ferrara

Bologna

Florence

Urbino

Siena

STATES OF

Perugia

THE CHURCH

Rome

Naples

School of
NAPLES

ROME
*Classicists
Mannerists
Caravaggio and
his followers
Baroque*

PIEDMONT

LOMBARDY

STATES OF THE CHURCH

KINGDOM OF NAPLES

SICILY

THE
ITALIAN
SCHOOLS
OF
PAINTING

Miles

0   50   100